Venus

CHERRY LAKE PRESS

Published in the United States of America by Cherry Lake Publishing
Ann Arbor, Michigan
www.cherrylakepublishing.com

Reading Adviser: Marla Conn, MS, Ed, Literacy specialist, Read-Ability, Inc.
Book Designer: Jennifer Wahl
Illustrator: Jeff Bane

Photo Credits: ©Vadim Sadovski/Shutterstock, 5, 21; ©Triff/Shutterstock, 7, 9; ©Nowwy Jirawat/Shutterstock, 11; ©NASA images/Shutterstock, 13, 15, 23; ©Midori9813/Shutterstock, 17; ©Withan Tor/Shutterstock, 19; Cover, 2-3, 8, 12, 22, Jeff Bane; Various vector images throughout courtesy of Shutterstock.com/

Library of Congress Cataloging-in-Publication Data

Names: Devera, Czeena, author. | Bane, Jeff, 1957- illustrator. | Devera, Czeena. My guide to the planets.
Title: Venus / by Czeena Devera ; illustrated by Jeff Bane.
Description: Ann Arbor, Michigan : Cherry Lake Publishing, [2020] | Series: My guide to the planets | Includes index. | Audience: K-1.
Identifiers: LCCN 2019032866 | ISBN 9781534158856 (hardcover) | ISBN 9781534161153 (paperback) | ISBN 9781534160002 (pdf) | ISBN 9781534162303 (ebook)
Subjects: LCSH: Venus (Planet)--Juvenile literature.
Classification: LCC QB621 .D48 2020 | DDC 523.42--dc23
LC record available at https://lccn.loc.gov/2019032866

Printed in the United States of America
Corporate Graphics

About the author: Czeena Devera grew up in the red-hot heat of Arizona surrounded by books. Her childhood bedroom had built-in bookshelves that were always full. She now lives in Michigan with an even bigger library of books.

About the illustrator: Jeff Bane and his two business partners own a studio along the American River in Folsom, California, home of the 1849 Gold Rush. When Jeff's not sketching or illustrating for clients, he's either swimming or kayaking in the river to relax.

I'm Venus. I am the closest planet to Earth.

I'm also similar to Earth in size. Some even say we're sisters!

I am called Evening and
Morning Star. I'm close
and bright!

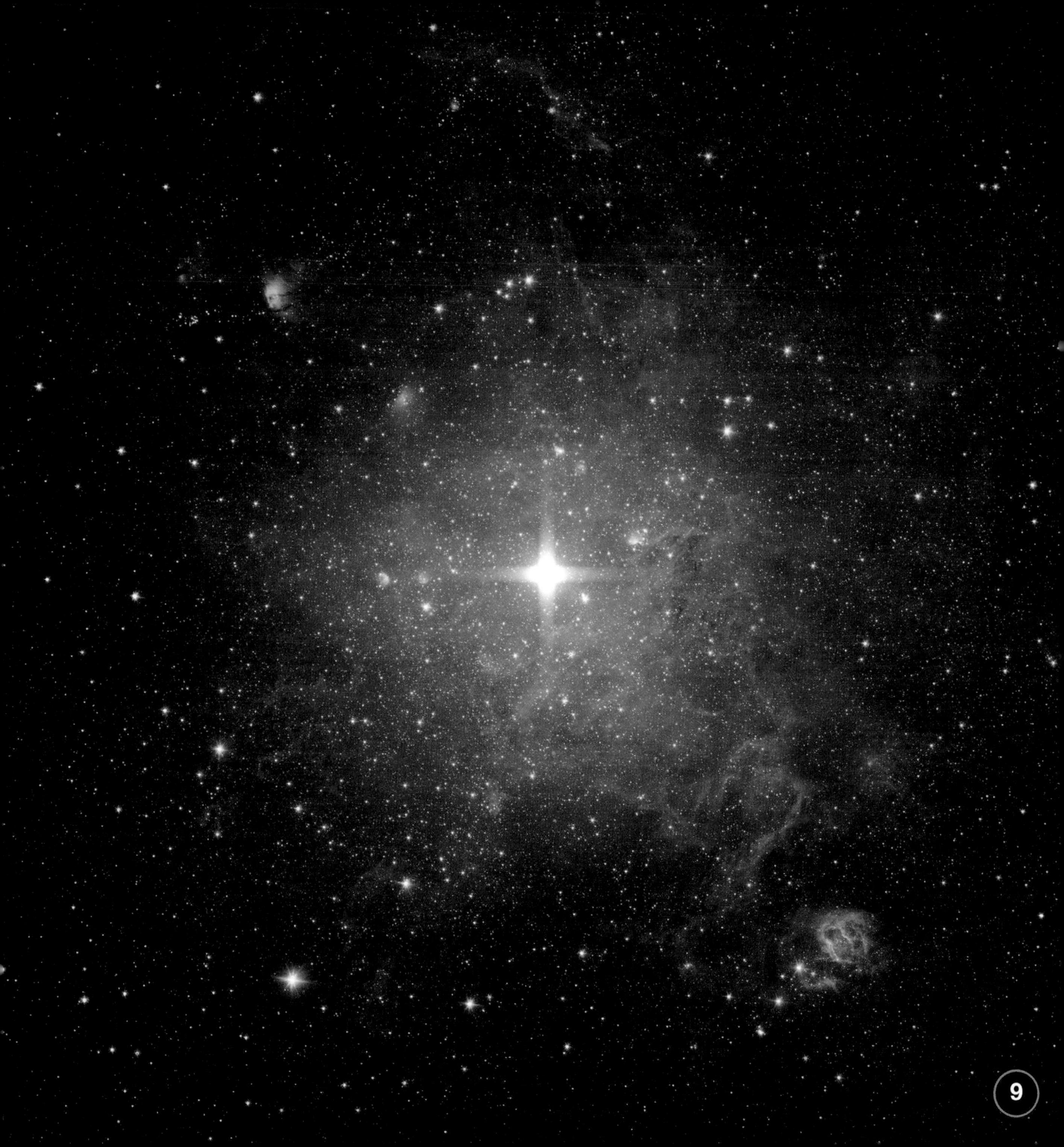

I can be seen from Earth on a clear night. I can be seen on clear days too.

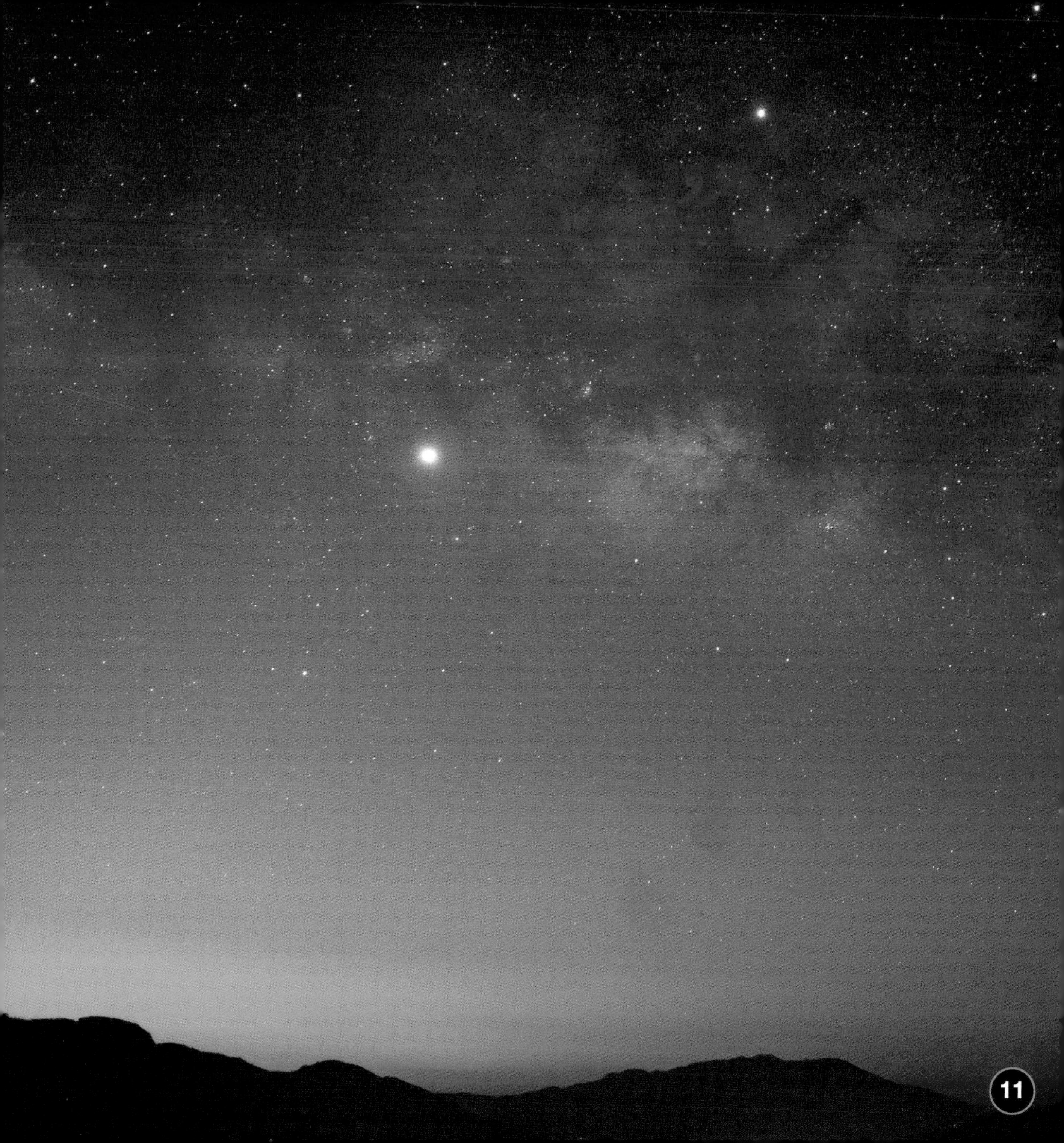

Which planet is the closest to the Sun?

I'm the second-closest planet to the Sun. I'm also the hottest.

I **orbit** around the Sun. It takes me 225 days to complete 1 orbit.

I **rotate** slowly. One complete day for me lasts 117 days on Earth!

I also rotate differently. I go in the opposite direction of most other planets.

I do not have any rings or moons.

I am a **unique** planet. There are new things about me being discovered.

glossary

orbit (OR-bit) to travel in a curved path around something

rotate (ROH-tate) to move in a circle around a central point, like a wheel

unique (yoo-NEEK) the only one of its kind

index